Tiny Tinkles Little Musicians Series

Yummy In My Tummy

Created by **Debra Krol**   Pictures by **Corinne Orazietti**

This book is dedicated to
all the little people for inspiring me,
and all the BIG people for believing in me.

Copyright © 2020 Tiny Tinkles Publishing Company

All Rights Reserved.

No parts of this publication or the characters in it, may be reproduced or distributed in any form or by any means without written permission from the publisher.

To request permission, or for school visits and book readings, please visit www.tinytinkles.com

ISBN (Paperback): 978-0-9808888-2-9

ISBN (Ebook): 978-0-9808888-3-6

First Edition 2020
Author/Creator: Debra Krol
Illustrations by: Corinne Orazietti
Editor: Tanya Guenther

HOW TO READ THIS BOOK

Read the story. Have fun! Use silly voices and make animal sounds.

Talk about what you see. Music notes, symbols and note names are scattered throughout the story. Point them out or ask your child to find them for more learning opportunities.

Tiny Tinkles Little Musician books are designed to grow with your child. Pages and concepts in this book can be used independently or read from cover to cover in one sitting. Introduce learning and concepts as your child is ready.

TOOLS TO HELP YOU TEACH

Music Road – When you see the dotted line of Music Road, follow it with your finger or have your child follow it with their finger. Make your voice higher or lower as the line moves up and down.

Animal Friends – All the animal friends correspond to music notes and each has their favorite letter. Point to the animal friends and find their favorite letters on the page, or sing their song (meow meow, woof woof etc. to reinforce music concepts and note memory.

Sing Along – When you see this star with the name of a song inside, you can sing along with a recording of the song. Go to tinytinkles.com to access the recordings.

Music Notes and their Values - Quarter Notes ♩ have one beat, Half Notes ♩ have two beats, and Whole Notes 𝅝 have four beats.

Pronunciations - musical terms are written in Italian. Mr. Fine's name is pronounced FEE-NAY and Bobby Bass is pronounced BACE, just like FACE.

For videos, worksheets, and other resources, please visit
www.tinytinkles.com

Today is the perfect day for a picnic in
Tiny Tinkles Town!

The sun is shining, and all the birds are singing.

Pink birds, blue birds, and owls all sing their special **songs**.

chirp   chirp

And together, they all sing in perfect **harmony**.

The pink birds sing a chirping **quarter note** song.

chirp chirp chirp chirp

And the owls sing a hooting **whole note** song.

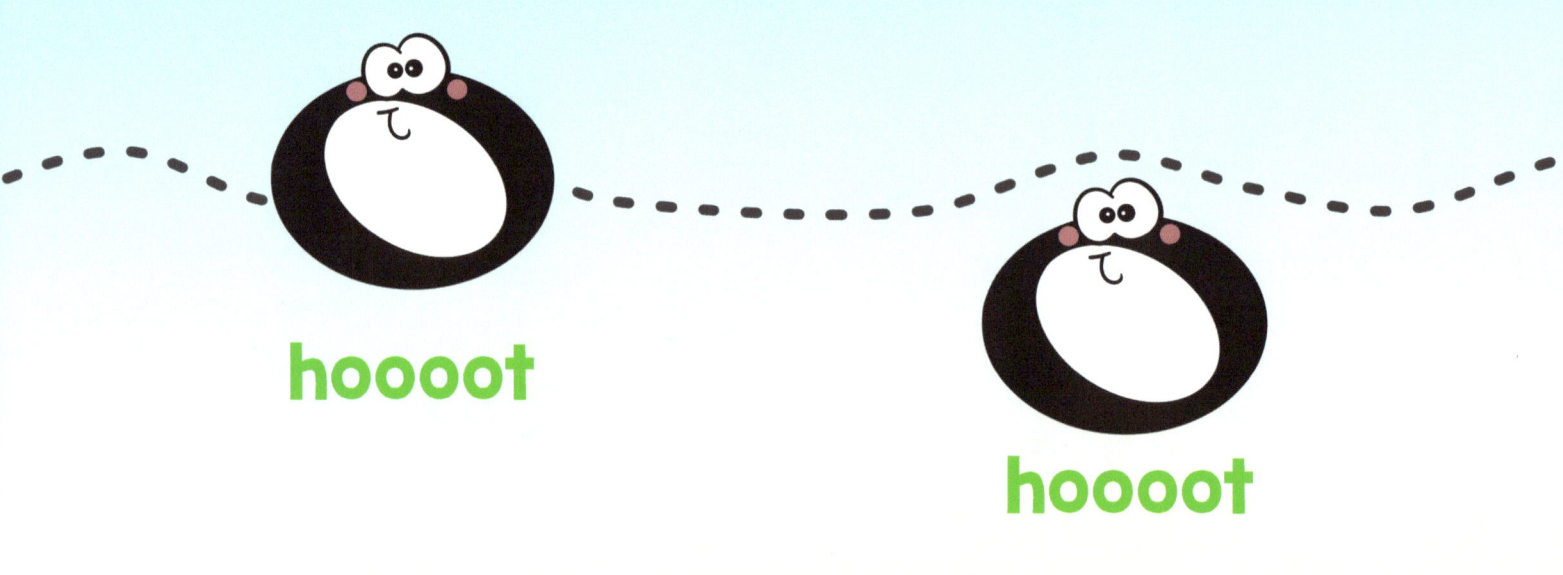

hoooot

hoooot

YUM! YUM!

What will Tina Treble and Bobby Bass bring?
Ice Cream Cones!

They tap their bellies and sing their song...

YUMMY in my TUMMY

mmm mmm GOOD.

YUM! YUM!

And what will Chloe Cat bring?

Crackers, Cheese and Sardines!

She taps her belly and sings her song...

YUM! YUM!

And what will Daisy Dog bring?
Dill Pickles and Peanut Butter!
She taps her belly and sings her song...

YUM! YUM!

And what will Elly Elephant bring?

Eggplant and Escargot!

She taps her belly and sings her song...

YUM! YUM!

And what will Franky Frog bring?
Fried Fish and Pretzel Sticks!
He taps his belly and sings his song...

YUM! YUM!

And what will Gordie Goat bring?
Gummy Worms and Granola

He taps his belly and sings his song...

YUM! YUM!

And what will Ally Alligator bring?
Animal Crackers and Avocados.
She taps her belly and sings her song...

YUM! YUM!

And what will Brownie Bear bring?
Broccoli and Blueberries!
She taps her belly and sings her song...

The picnic is **perfect!** Together the friends eat and sing, again and again.

meow   woof   pahwoo

When they are all done and their bellies are full,
Mr. Fine sings **"THE END."**

ribbit   maa   chomp   ROAR!

The End.

Quarter, Half and Whole Notes

tap tap tap tap

tap some notes are

SHORT

and some notes

HOLD
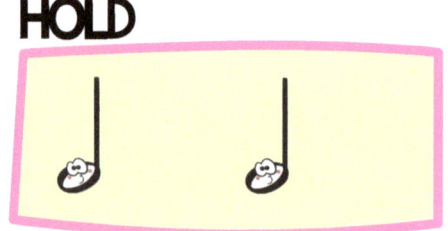

some notes are

SHORT

and some notes

HOLD

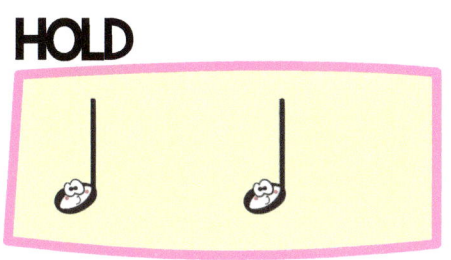  

meow meow meow meow

meow meow meow meow

woof woof

woof woof

pahwoo   pahwoo

hop,   rib bit   hop,   rib bit

maa maa maa   maa maa maa.

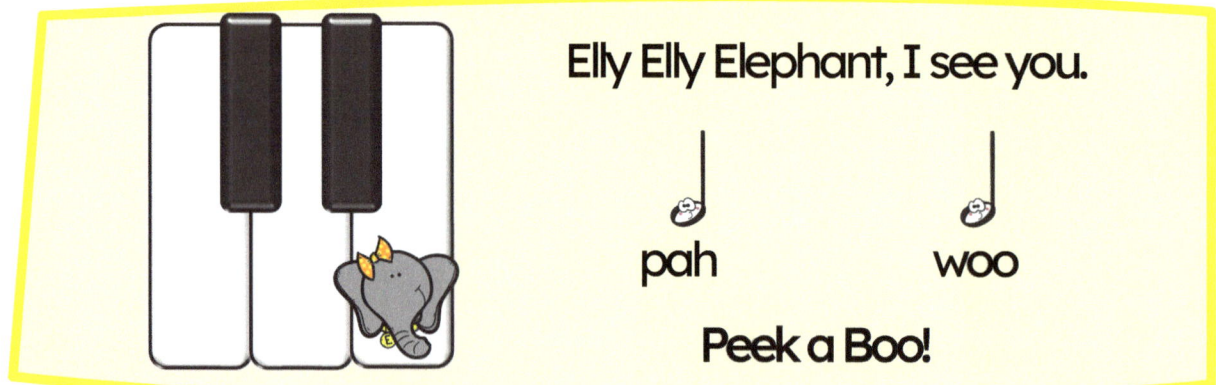

1, 2... I see you. I see a group of 2!

1, 2, 3... Count with me. I see a group of 3!

Game Card Cutting Instructions:

Watch a video with these instructions on our website www.tinytinkles.com

1. **Cut** the RED line first.
2. **LAMINATE** the page. (If laminating isn't an option, use a glue stick to glue each card to a sheet of card stock)
3. **Cut** into individual cards.
4. **Tape the Yummy In My Tummy POCKET** to the INSIDE, back cover of the book. Place the tape around the sides and the bottom. Leave the top open so you can place your cards inside the pocket when not in use.

Game Ideas and Instructions:

1. **Cover** up the animals in the **Peek A Boo Song** with the Star Cards and guess who is underneath. It's ok to peek if you do not know who's under the card!
2. **Cover** the black key groups with the Numbered Star Cards.
3. **Cover** the white keys with the correct Animal Cards.
4. **SORT** the Note Cards into categories.
5. **COMPOSITION ACTIVITY:** Make your own songs with the Note Cards. Place your favorite Animal Card in front of "your song" and try singing with the correct rhythm and using your favorite friends sound.
6. **SORT** the Piano Keys into groups of 2 black keys and 3 black keys.
7. **PIANO PUZZLE:** Arrange the groups of Piano Keys in an alternating pattern of 2 black keys and 3 black keys.
8. **MATCHING Animals:** Use the Animal Cards to practice matching the Animals in the songs with their correct cards.
9. **MATCHING:** Match the Note cards with the correct number of Counting Star Cards.
10. **MEMORY:** Play a game with the Note Cards and collect the pairs.

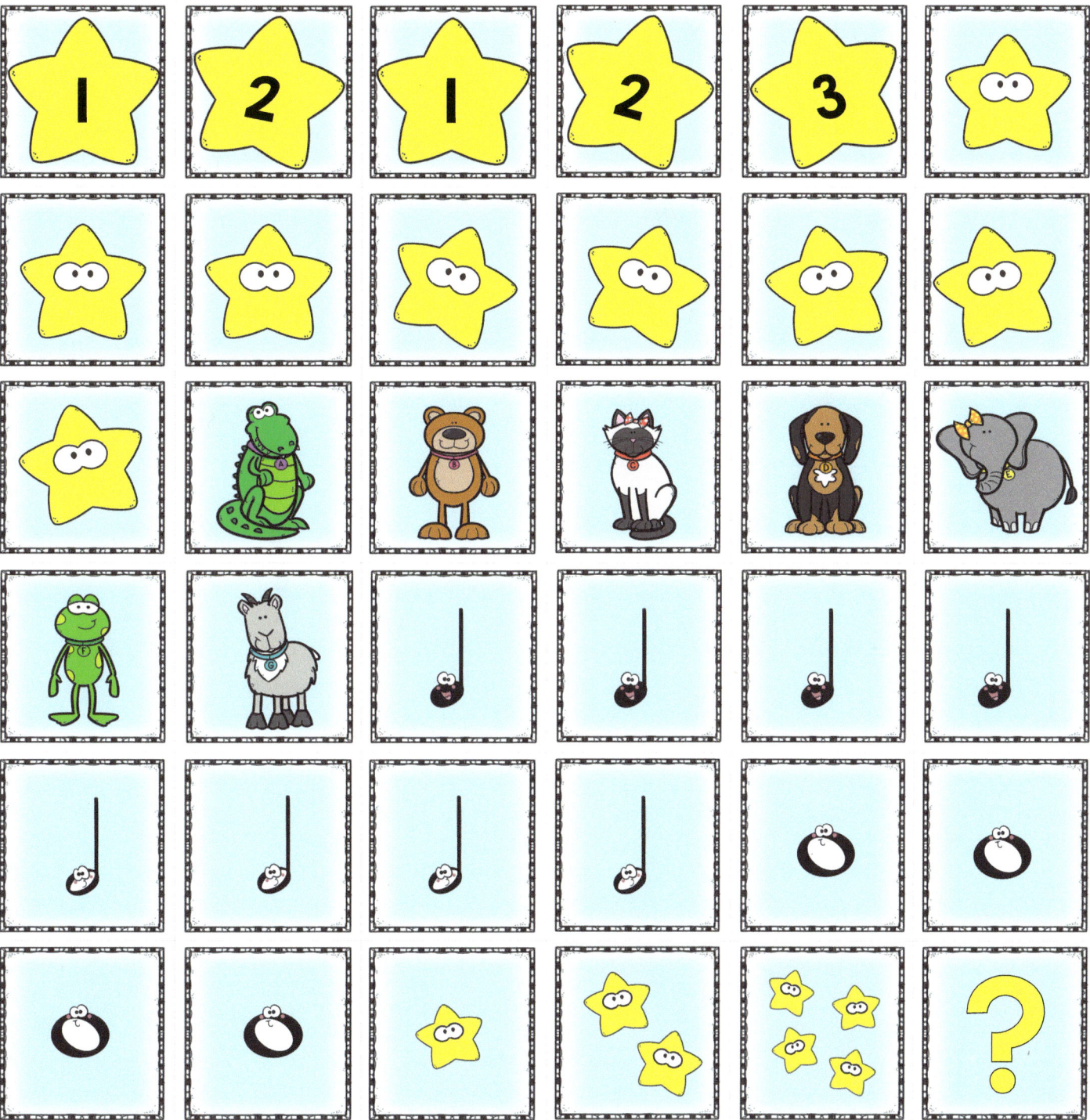

background by @hidesysclipart

ABOUT THE CREATORS

Debra Krol is a BC Registered Music Teacher who specializes in teaching music to babies, toddlers and preschoolers. She is also a children's songwriter and author. Ms. Deb enjoys camping with her hubby, kids, and Daisy Dog, their black and tan coonhound. She loves playing piano, ukulele, guitar and most of all, singing & drawing with all of her little friends!

 Tiny Tinkles Music Studio   tinytinkles

Corinne Orazietti was a preschool and elementary teacher for many years. She saw how her whimsical illustrations added sparkle to her lessons and decided it was time to share her passion for art with others. She now works as a full-time artist at her company, Chirp Graphics, and spends her days drawing cartoon dragons and fairies.

 chirpgraphics   chirpgraphicsclipart

ABOUT THE SERIES

The **Tiny Tinkles Little Musicians Series** was created to help little musicians experience the FUN of learning music. After all, in Tiny Tinkles Town, music comes in every color of the rainbow!

Every book in the Little Musician series features a Story to read, Songs to sing and play, and a ton of fun Games to play together! When a child plays to learn, they learn to play.

We are GROWING! More books in the Series available in 2021.

www.ingramcontent.com/pod-product-compliance
Lightning Source LLC
Chambersburg PA
CBHW042140290426
44110CB00002B/72